The Lady of Heaven

The Lady of Heaven

ALDIVAN TORRES

aldivan teixeira torres

CONTENTS

The Lady of Heaven
  Aldivan Teixeira Torres
The Lady of Heaven
Author: Aldivan Teixeira Torres
© 2018-Aldivan Teixeira Torres
All rights reserved

Aldivan Teixeira Torres is a consolidated writer in several genres. To date, titles have been published in nine languages. From an early age, he was always a lover of the art of writing having consolidated a professional career from the second semester of 2013. He hopes with his writings to contribute to the Pernambuco and Brazilian culture, awakening the pleasure of reading in those who do not yet have the habit. Its mission is to win the hearts of each of its readers. In addition to literature, his main tastes are music, travel, friends, family, and the pleasure of living. "For literature, equality, fraternity, justice, dignity, and honor of the human being always" is his motto.

Our lady appeared
Our Lady of Aparecida
Known miracles of Our Lady appeared
Our Lady of the Presentation

Our lady appeared

Barcelos-portugal-1702

It was August 1702. Young John was pastoring his flock on Monte de Castro de Balugães when a storm broke out. Looking for shelter in a cave in a limpet, he was surprised due to the appearance of a beautiful lady enveloped in light.

"Why are you surprised, John?" The woman asked.

"I am terrified because I have never seen an apparition," replied the ex-mute, being instantly cured.

"Calm down, young man." I am Our Lady. I ask you to send a message to your father that I want the construction of a Chapel in this place.

"He is well. I'll give you the message now — John readied himself.

"Thank you very much." She thanked Our Mother.

The young man ran towards his house full of joy. For him, it was an honor to have been chosen as a spokesman for that saint so dear to the Christian community. It was prudent, then, to fulfill his wish as soon as possible.

Arriving home, he found his father resting on the sofa in the living room. He took the opportunity to start a conversation.

"Father, I need to speak to you."

"What? Weren't you dumb?

"I was healed." Can you hear me?

"Yes, you can talk.

"I have a request to make: I want you to build a Chapel in honor of Our Lady of Aparecida.

"Where did you get this idea from, boy?"

"It was the saint who asked."

"Saint?" Can you explain this story better?

"She came to me when I was with my flock at Monte De Castro de Balugães." It was obvious in your request.

"You drank? Where have you ever seen spirits? I already know: You drank, dreamed and thought it was all real.

"But dad!

"I don't believe this. Conversation ended!

The young man was saddened for the rest of the day. The next day, she went back to herding in the same place as before. That was when the strange Lady appeared again.

"How are you, John?" Did you follow my orders?

"Yes, my mother. However, it was no use. My father did not believe my words.

"How insensitive of him!" Go home and reiterate my request. To convince him, ask him for bread.

"Okay, ma'am." I will do as you ask.

The boy hurried home again. At this moment, curiosity reigned over what was going to happen relates his request, as they usually had no bread available on this day. Even so, he would obey the saint's order.

John had always been a quiet and ordinary boy, but after the last events he had become inexplicably mysterious and enlightened. This change was credited with the great work of God in his life.

When he got home, he found his father resting in the same place as before. Then he approached again.

"Father, the saint appeared to me again." She requests the construction of her Chapel once more.

"This story again?" Haven't you tired of it yet?

"Since you didn't believe her, she says: Give me bread.

"Bread? I have none with me. If you want crumbs, I have some in the oven.

"Go get it for me."

Grudgingly, you got up and went to check. When he opened the oven, what was his surprise when he saw it full of bread.

"So says our mother: just as I converted crumbs into bread, I can also convert your hard heart."

"My God and my mother!" How foolish I was not to believe. I promise to carry out Our mother's request urgently.

"Good, my father." Write to the bishop. He will help us.

"Good idea.

They communicated the facts to the Diocese which, through investigation, proved them. The Virgin Mother temple was built where the same boy worked as a sexton until the end of his days. With the appearance in Barcelos, Our Lady became the special protector of the Portuguese people.

Our Lady of Aparecida

Aparecida-Brasil-1717

It was the second half of October 1717. Pedro Miguel de Almeida Portugal and Vasconcelos, Count of Assumar and Governor of the captaincy of São Paulo and Gold mines were visiting Guaratinguetá. To honor them, some groups of fishermen launched their boats in the Paraíba River to catch fish.

Among them, fishermen Domingos Garcia, John Alves and Filipe Pedroso prayed to the Virgin Mary asking for divine help. There were several unsuccessful fishing attempts until, near the Port of Itaguaçu, they fished the image of the Virgin Mary. In later attempts, they caught so much fish that the vessel could barely carry their weight.

The image was lodged in Filipe Pedroso's residence for fifteen years from where he received a visit from the faithful for prayer. There were many reports of miracles, which attracted more and more people from all parts of the country. The solution was to transfer the image to an oratory and later a chapel was built that became the basilica of today, the fourth most visited Marian Temple in the world.

On July 16, 1930, Our Lady of Conception of Aparecida was proclaimed the patron saint of Brazil by Pope Pius XI. The October 12 holiday was made official by Law number 6802, dated June 30, 1980. Our Lady of Aparecida is the protector of all Brazilians.

Known miracles of Our Lady appeared

Miracle of the Candles-1733

It was a quiet night in the oratory that housed the image of the saint. For no apparent reason, the two candles that lit the place went out. Before they could rekindle them, they ignited by themselves causing great admiration among those present.

Fall of the Chains-1850

A slave named Zacarias, passing near the Church where the image of the saint was, asked permission from the overseer to enter the temple and pray to Our Lady. Granted, he enters the sanctuary and kneels before the image, praying fervently. Before ending the prayer, miraculously the chains that bound him loosen, leaving him completely free.

The Knight

A knight, passing through Aparecida, very skeptical of God, made fun of the pilgrims when he saw their faith. Wanting to prove his hypothesis, he promised himself to go horseback riding into the Church. Before, however, achieving his intent, his horse's paw was caught in the stone of the Church's staircase, knocking him down. Thereafter, he repented and became a devotee of the Virgin.

The blind

The Vaz family lived in Jaboticabal, and they were all very devoted to Our Lady of Aparecida. Among the family members, the youngest girl was blind from birth. She had great faith in Our Lady and her greatest dream was to visit the basilica of the saint.

Through the work of the Holy Spirit, the family fulfilled the girl's dream during the vacation period. Suddenly, when she reached the steps of the Church, the girl exclaimed: "Mother, how beautiful this Church is!" From this day on, she began to see normally, increasing the number of miracles attributed to the patron saint of Brazil.

The boy in the river

The son and his father went to the river to fish. This was a routine activity for both with them already having experience in it. Even so, an accident occurred: Due to the strong current, the boy fell into the river being dragged by the current. Desperate, the father cried out for the help of Our Lady of Aparecida. Immediately, the current calmed what allowed the boy's salvation through his father.

The man and the jaguar

A farmer was on his way home after a normal day of toil. At one point, a jaguar appeared that scared and cornered him. The way out was to call for help to Our Lady of Aparecida. The strategy worked because the jaguar simply ran away.

Our Lady of the Presentation

Natal-Brasil-1753

On November 21, 1753, fishermen found a wooden crate on one of the rocks near the Potengi River Bank. Upon opening the box, they found an image of Our Lady of Rosario accompanied by the following message: Where this image brings no misfortune will happen.

The city priest was informed of the discovery and as this day was exactly the date on which Mary was presented to the temple in Jerusalem, the image was baptized as "Our Lady of the Presentation" and proclaimed the city's patron. This day is a holiday in the city, a day of devotion to the saintly protector of all North — Rio Grande do Sul.

Our Lady of Lavang

Vietnam-1798

At the end of the 18th century, there was a dispute between the various competitors for the Vietnamese throne. Among them, Nguyen Anh, requested support from Catholics and the monarch of France. Knowing this, Canh Thin, his opponent, ordered the destruction of all Catholic entities that supported him.

The way out for the small group of Christians in that country was to take refuge in the mountains between the borders. However, his opponents did not rest to annihilate them. In addition, they suffered from hunger, cold, disease, and attacks by wild animals. It was in this extreme situation that one day Our Lady appeared to a group of people in a long white dress with the baby Jesus in her arms and surrounded by angels. She then contacted them.

"I am Our Lady." My heart is with you in this difficult situation. Do not be discouraged! Take Lavang leaves, boil them and have tea. In this way, they will be cured of their illnesses. I also promise to listen to all the prayers made in this place.

That said, it disappeared like smoke. In this place, a simple chapel was erected. It was the meeting point for the faithful who fled persecution. During almost a hundred years of religious persecution, the saint appeared on this site several times giving instructions and encouraging them. Our Lady of Lavang thus became the special protector of Vietnamese Christians.

Our Lady of Lichen

1850-Poland

It was 1813. At that time, there was a revolution taking over Europe brought about by Napoleon and his soldiers. As in any war, there were huge human losses to consider. We can take as an example the battle of the nations in which about eighty thousand combatants were wounded.

Among so many soldiers, one of them named Tomasz Klossowski was devoted to Our Lady. Every night, he insisted on the request that he not die in foreign lands. On one of those fervent nights, the immaculate one appeared to him wearing a golden robe and a white eagle in his hand.

"I am Our Lady." I heard your prayers. You will return to your region. When that happens, look for an image like me and spread my devotion.

"Thank you very much, my mother." I'm happy with the news. I will do it according to your holy will.

"I am happy, good servant." I leave you my peace. Go ahead and let this war end soon.

"So be it!

The mother of us all rose before her eyes and soon disappeared into the immensity of the heavens. Miraculously, this servant was saved from all dangers in battles and at the end of them he returned to his home region. Over the course of twenty-three years, he searched for the said image and ended up finding it. He placed it in his home and later in a chapel located in a nearby forest.

However, despite her efforts, Mary's devotion did not become popular in the region, leaving the image abandoned in the forest. On August 15, 1850, the saint manifested herself to a pastor who was passing by.

"I am Our Lady." I am sorrowful about the desolation of this image and concerned about the evil that contaminates the world. People sin continuously, do not think about doing penance and changing their lives. It won't be long, and they will be severely punished by God for that. They will suddenly fall dead and there will be no one to bury them. Old people will die, children will die in the act of being fed by their mothers. Boys and girls will be punished, little orphans will cry their parents. Then there will be a long and terrible war.

"Couldn't you cry out to God to at least ease these woes?" — Mikolaj Sikatka asked.

"I do this all the time." Heavenly Father's mercy is inexhaustible, and everything can still be changed. When there are saints in the country, it can be saved. The country needs holy mothers. I love your good mothers; I will always help you in every need. I understand them: I was a mother, in a lot of pain.

"You're right. Poland really has extraordinary mothers. How can we repay their affection?

"The most perfidious intentions of the oppressors, your mothers break them. They give the country numerous and heroic children. In the period of a universal fire, these children will snatch the free homeland and in their own way will save them.

"I am happy. It was the least we could do.

"This is just a tip of the Iceberg." Evil does not rest. An example of this is that Satan will sow discord among the brethren. All the wounds will not be healed yet, and a generation will not grow until the land, the air, and the seas are covered with so much blood that until today it has not been seen. This land will be impregnated with tears, ash, and the blood of martyrs of the holy cause. In the heart of the country, youth will perish at the stake of sacrifice. Innocent children will die by the sword. These new and countless martyrs will plead before the throne of God's justice for you, when the final battle for the soul of the nation takes place, when you will be judged. In the fire of long trials faith will be purified, hope will not disappear, love will not cease. I will walk among you, I will defend you, I will help you, through you, I will help the world.

"Blessed be, my mother." Can we hope for a happy ending to this story?

"To the surprise of all nations, from Poland, hope will arise for tormented humanity. Then all hearts will move with joy, as there was not a thousand years ago. This will be the greatest signal given to the nation, for it to come to its senses and to comfort itself. It will unite you. Then, in that tormented and humiliated country, exceptional graces will descend as there were not a thousand years ago. Young hearts will move.

Seminars and convents will be full. Polish hearts will expand faith in the east and in the west, in the north and in the south. God's peace had been established.

"Glory to God!

"I have a special request to make: I want people to come together in prayer by praying my rosary. Likewise, I want priests to celebrate Mass with greater commitment. Regarding the image, I ask you to transfer it to a more suitable place. In the future, a monastery and sanctuary dedicated to me will be built. Because they are so dedicated to my cause, I will cover them with blessings and glories. Nothing can do you any harm.

"I will do what I can, my mother." You can rest easy.

"I know, good servant. I leave my peace with you!

"Thanks!

The angels surrounded Our Lady carrying her by the arms. Then they flew in the direction of the cosmos. The pastor was thoughtful for a few moments about the best strategy to be adopted in that situation. He ended up deciding to follow exactly the steps taken.

Time passed. Despite all the effort made by the servant, no one paid any attention to him. With his arrest, the situation worsened. The people only recognized the messages of the mother of God after a cholera epidemic. With that, they did penance. A commission was also set up whose main objective was to verify the veracity of the apparition. The conclusion of this process was positive.

The image was transferred several times until it was definitively in the seventh largest Church in Europe, the glory of its region. As time went by, devotion to the Virgin Mother of God increased in the country, which made the name of Mary all over Europe. Our Lady of Lichen is the special protector of all Poles.

Our Lady of Lourdes

France-1858

First apparition

February 11, 1858-A Thursday

Bernadete, her sister Marie and a friend were sent to the field to pick up dry branches. Usually, they willingly did this job, which gave them the feeling of being useful. Heading to this task, they agreed to go further, more precisely, until the meeting of the canal water and the Gave.

At the exact moment of the crossing of the water, next to a cave, the two companies of Bernardete started to cross the water while the same one was in doubt if it could do that too. This is explained by a medical recommendation not to take a cold.

After about five minutes, he finally took courage and started taking off his socks. It was at that very moment that he heard a noise similar to the wind. Looking at the opposite side of the cave, he noticed the standing trees, which calmed him down a little. Then he resumed the exercise of removing his socks.

Shortly afterwards, when he raised his head in the direction of the cave, he saw a madam dressed all in white. According to his description, in addition to the dress, she had a white veil, a blue belt, a rose on each foot and held a third. Frightened, the girl tried to take her third and make the sign of the cross, but was unsuccessful on the first attempt. With a little more time, it became more peaceful. He managed to make the sign of the cross and started praying the rosary.

Throughout the prayer, the strange lady remained attainable his eyes enigmatically. At the end of this religious activity, the apparition signaled for him to approach. Fear, however, prevented him. Realizing the girl's fragility, the beautiful lady moved away and disappeared into the immensity of the cave.

Alone, the dear girl finished taking off her shoes. He crossed the water to meet his companions. Afterwards, they harvested the dry branches and started to return home. Bothered by everything that had happened, she got in touch with the others.

"Did you see anything?"

"No, I didn't. Did you see something, Marie?" The friend asked.

"I didn't see it either." What did you see, sister? "Marie asked.

"If you haven't seen it, I haven't seen it either," Bernardete said.

The strange conversation made the other girls totally suspicious. So, on the way, they kept asking him questions. They insisted so much that the psychic had no choice but to tell.

"He is well. I saw a lady with a rosary in her hand in the cave. We spent a while admiring ourselves and praying the rosary.

"Who was it, sister?"" Marie asked.

"I didn't have the heart to ask." The fear was very great — Bernadette justified.

"I should have asked." Only in this way would we not be in doubt," observed Marie.

"Interesting! What a pity we didn't have a visa! "The friend was sorry."

"Do you keep this a secret?" Bernardete asked.

"Do not worry. Our mouths are like a grave," said the friend.

"Exactly! No one should know," said Marie.

The conversation ended and the girls continued to follow the route. When they got home, they didn't keep their promise by telling the story of the apparition to everyone. This was in short, the story of the first appearance.

Second appearance

February 14, 1858, a Sunday

Returning to the same place in the company of other girls, Bernardete took a bottle of holy water with him. Bravely, they entered the grotto and started praying. At the very beginning of this activity, the strange lady again appeared in the vision of the seer.

Instinctively, the clairvoyant started throwing holy water at the apparition saying:

"If you come from God, stay. If not, go away.

The vision smiled and nodded without saying anything, which added to the drama of the situation. After all, who was she, and what was she looking for? Holy water was poured into it until the end. When the rosary is completed, the woman mysteriously disappeared. With that, that group of young people returned to their respective homes.

Third apparition

February 18, 1858, One Thursday

Returning to the place with people belonging to the elite, the seer took ink and paper with her, following the advice of some. At the beginning of the prayer of the rosary, the woman appeared again. The first contact was then made.

"If you have anything to say, say I'll be taking notes," Bernadette said.

"There is no need to write what I have to say." However, do you want to have the grace to visit me here for fifteen days?

"Yes," the servant of God said.

"I'm glad for your decision." Continue the prayer with great faith. I will always be blessing you," said the apparition.

"Amen," the little girl wanted.

They continued in the prayer of the rosary and at the end of it the vision again disappeared. The mystery remained and then those in the cave returned home.

Fourth apparition

February 19, 1858, a Friday

The psychic and about six friends entered the cave searching for the mysterious woman. When beginning the prayer of the third, from the third bird Mary, the sight of the strange lady is obvious and lasts for about thirty minutes. It is long enough for her to convey some secret guidelines of devotion. When the rosary is completed, it mysteriously disappears. As agreed, the prophet and friends promise to return the next day.

Fifth appearance

February 20, 1858

Soon, Bernadette and thirty other witnesses arrived at the cave. As soon as the prayers began, the lady of heaven revealed herself to be the servant. The lesson of the day was to teach him a prayer that should be kept secret. After finishing this task, they said goodbye. Another day had been accomplished.

Sixth apparition

February 21, 1858

Bernadette returned to the cave with a contingent of one hundred people. At seven o'clock in the morning, the glorious madam introduced herself:

"Good Morning! May peace be with you!

"So be it. What do you want for today?

"I came to advise you to stay on your path." In particular, pray for sinners.

"I'll do it. But sometimes people are so rude and insensitive.

"It is true. However, God can do anything. He asks for your cooperation.

"I feel grateful for this invitation." I don't want anything in return for that.

"You don't want to, but God will give it to you." I promise you happiness.

"On here? In this sea of evil?

"I promise you security and peace on earth." Happiness will be achieved in the heavens.

"Let it be done to me according to your words."

"Amen! Peace and good! I have to go now.

"Go in peace!

Fading into the darkness of the cave, the enlightened one left the servants to pray. Certainly, more blessing would be sent by that being of pure light.

Leaving the cave with the crowd, the psychic started her return home. At this point in history, the apparitions were already known to many people, which generated more and more rumors.

One of those who had learned of this fact, was the city delegate Dominique Jacomet. He was a brute man who disbelieved religions, striving for good public order. The repercussions of the apparitions were so strong that he was forced to investigate the case. With that, the clairvoyant was called to testify.

As a citizen fulfilling her duties, she answered her summons knowing that she had nothing to fear. On the afternoon of the same day, she visited the officer at work. Gathering in a private room, she began to be questioned.

"Miss, I have called you here to clarify." It is known in the whole community of the probable apparitions. What do you say about that? The delegate asked.

"I am honored to have been chosen by the forces of heaven." It doesn't magnify me or ennoble me at all. I'm just part of a bigger plan," replied the interviewee.

"What? Are you trying to convince me that this is true? Soon to me?

"No wonder I can believe it." After all, God can do anything.

"Foolishness! I don't believe in fairies, goblins, black-faced ox or even spirits! Isn't it enough for me to worry about the processes? Will I also have to take care of alienates now?

"It is no alienation." And only the action of God!

"He arrives! I have already drawn my own conclusions! From now on, I forbid you to return to the cave.

"But what am I doing wrong?"

"I just don't want it to become something bigger." Go home and obey.

"I respect your authority, but I cannot promise that.

"You are warned." If you insist, you will have to bear the consequences. Agenda closed!

Bernadete left the room and the police station. The audience with the deputy had made him uneasy. However, he carried in his chest the certainty that no man could be greater than God. I would think about something about it. Arriving home and talking about the interview with the deputy, the father scolded her strongly forbidding her access to the cave. The young woman burst into tears because she knew that everything would be more difficult relates her pretensions.

Seventh Appearance

February 22, 1858

The delegate was convinced of his decision. Aiming to carry out his orders, he placed soldiers to garrison the cave. Although it was forbidden, the brave girl insisted on the promise made to God. Miraculously, the opponents were unaware of her presence and she can enter that sacred place. As usual, he prayed in a low voice. However, nothing happened. This time, the visit had not arrived. Returning to the city, he learned of the suspension of the ban. This was a personal victory for Christ against Satan.

Eighth Apparition

February 24, 1858

It was a warm and peaceful Wednesday. Near the grotto, there were about three hundred people. The Antichrist shouted against the crowd.

"How is it possible that there are still so many idiots in the middle of the 19th century?"

In response, the Marian devotees sang songs in honor of the Virgin. Bernadette is ecstatic for a few moments. Usually, it is at these times that you receive messages. Turning to the crowd, the venerable woman calls out:

"Penance, penance, penance!" Pray to God for the conversion of sinners!

In tears, the crowd promised to comply with the request. The dark forces had lost yet another battle against the power of Our Lady. The figure of her stepping on a snake represents the hope of the humble in God. Blessed be our mother!

Ninth apparition

February 25, 1858

The seer and three hundred more people are near the cave when the apparition appears.

"Good morning, my beloved friend." Your task today is to go to the source and wash yourself. You will eat the grass that is there.

"I'll do this now," said the dear servant.

The clairvoyant did as request by the saint. The vision disappeared and the young woman was forced to give up the day's work. Appearing before the crowd that waited anxiously, they asked:

"Do you know who thinks you're crazy about doing these things?"

"It is for sinners," replies the venerable devotee.

With the matter closed, they each returned to their respective homes.

Tenth apparition

February 27, 1858

About eight hundred people attend this act. Bernadette drinks holy water, penances and makes prayer chains. The strange lady observes all of this in silence.

Eleventh appearance

February 28, 1858

The audience grows every day. Now there are a thousand people watching the seer going into ecstasy, praying, kissing the earth and on their knees as a sign of mortification. Due to the repercussion of these acts, she is taken before the judge and the same are threatened with imprisonment. Again, the forces of darkness were trying to hinder the path of this disciple of Christ.

Twelfth apparition

March 1, 1858

The fame of the apparitions grew more and more. As a result, the audience for that day exceeded five thousand people. The same ritual as the other times followed, with the power of light accompanying everything. With the departure of all, Catarina Latapie, a friend of the seer, went to the cave believing in the miraculous power of the fountain that is found there. By wetting the diseased arm, the arm, and hand are mysteriously healed resulting in a return of movements. There was proof that God was working in that place.

Thirteenth appearance

March 2, 1858

The crowd increases considerably. As soon as the chain of prayers begins, the madam appears.

"Good morning, my dearest friend." I have a request today: You are going to tell the priests to come here in procession and to build a chapel.

"Good Morning! I'll get the message across now.

Moving to the group of priests, she gets in touch.

"The lady who appears to me asks that they organize a procession to this place and that a chapel be built.

"I demand two things for this: I want to know the name of that Lady and see a miracle. I will not believe it until the rose bush blooms — Peyramale replied.

"I will pass on your demands, dear priest," Bernadette agreed.

Returning to the apparition, he asks, but the vision remains silent. Shortly after, it disappears, saddening all the audience. It hadn't been this time yet.

Fourteenth apparition

March 3, 1858

In the morning, the seer comes to the cave accompanied by about three thousand people. Although all the ritual steps have been followed to the letter, the vision does not appear leaving a little frustration in people. Later, the seer receives a message from the woman asking for her return to the cave. There, it manifests itself again. Following the priest's request, the young woman asks the same question as always. In response, he receives a smile. When she leaves the cave, she comes back in contact with the priest who reiterates his demand: "If she really wants a chapel, let her tell her name and make the rose bush bloom in the middle of winter".

The blessed young woman returns home full of hopes of seeing this miracle fulfilled. After all, there is nothing impossible with God.

Fifteenth apparition

March 4, 1858

The crowd grows considerably: Now there are eight thousand people looking for a personal answer to the dazzling sight. Contrary to all expectations, the woman remains silent in the face of all questions. The mystery surrounding this figure was getting bigger and bigger. For twenty days, Bernadette does not return to the cave.

Sixteenth apparition

March 25, 1858

It was a calm and warm morning when the girl again entered the cave. As usual, he began to say the rosary. In this, the enlightened one appeared.

"I am here again. Have faith in God and me. I am called the Immaculate Conception.

"I have a lot of faith." I will pass on your message to the priests.

Running happily, the servant of God told the priests what had happened. They are impressed; therefore, the title "Immaculate Conception" had been given as an honor to Our Lady and considered as a dogma. The mystery was therefore solved.

Seventeenth apparition

April 7, 1858

In front of the crowd, Bernadette lights the candle. His hand was engulfed in flames during this process. At the end of this act, it was found that she did not suffer any burns, increasing the list of miracles of the Immaculate Virgin.

Eighteenth apparition

Access to the cave was forbidden to the unhappiness of all the faithful of Our Lady. Alternatively, Bernadette uses another route to approach the site. His vision is of Our Lady of Mount Carmel waving goodbye. This cycle of apparitions was thus ended.

Conclusion

Four years later, the visions were said to be authentic. The seer entered the congregation of the daughters of charity where she stayed until her death. His canonization took place on December 8, 1933.

Our Lady of Good Help

October 9, 1859

Champion Wisconsin-USA

Nun Adele and other neighbors fetched wheat from Champion. At one point, she was surprised by the appearance of a woman standing between two trees. The lady wore white robes, her hair was auburn, her dark, deep eyes powerfully fixed on the young woman. Filled with fear, our sister in Christ kept thinking about what she should do until the vision simply disappeared. She then returned to the convent.

Later, passing through the same place, he saw the image again. Upon arriving at the convent, still frightened, she revealed the secret to her personal confessor:

"Father, a woman has appeared to me twice. What should I do?

"Get in touch with her." If you're from heaven, it won't hurt you.

"He is well!

Following his advice, the nun returned to the apparition site. As expected, he appeared to the same lady. Calmer, she interviewed the vision.

"Who, is it? And what do you want from me?

"I am the Queen of Heaven, who prays for the conversion of sinners, and I wish you to do the same. You received Holy Communion this morning, and you are well. But you must do more. Make a general Confession and offer Communion for the conversion of sinners. If they do not convert and do penance, my Son will be obliged to punish them. Happy are those who believe without seeing. What are you doing here in idleness while your companions are working in my Son's vineyard? Gather the children of this wild country and teach them what they must know for their salvation. Teach them the Catechism, how to make the Sign of the Cross and approach the Sacraments. This is what I wish you to do. Go and don't be afraid. I will help.

"I am honored to have delivered such a glorious mission." Blessed be among all women!

"Blessed be our God!"

"I will do as you ask."

"Be at peace then!" May we join our forces so that more sinners are converted! I don't want to lose any of these little ones.

"Me neither! Thank you, my mother.

"You're welcome, daughter."

That said, the madame rose to her sight, going to join the angels in heaven. This was another one of the recorded apparitions aiming at its greatest glory. Blessed be our mother.

Our Lady of Hope

Pontmain-France-1871

At around six o'clock on the 17th of January, Eugênio Barbeie-took care of his younger brother. At this moment, the neighbor named Joana Details had arrived. She came to talk a little and miss her dear friends. With the interruption of his duties, Eugênio wanted to go out for a while and he did so.

At this moment, he was surprised to see a lady floating a few meters above a neighboring house. The beautiful woman shone like the sun. His garment was blue adorned with shining stars, and his pair of shoes were blue with gold buckles. In addition, he wore a black veil carefully overlaid with a gold crown on his head.

The boy admired the figure for a while. Shortly after, the neighbor also went outside, and he took advantage of the situation to talk to her.

"Joan, don't you see anything up there in the smoke shop?" The child asked, pointing with his index finger at the sight.

"I don't see anything, my son," said the neighbor flatly.

In this, the boy's parents also leave, but they cannot see anything. The younger boy sees the same image. The others do not believe their versions and force them to enter the house for dinner. Later, he gets a license to leave again. There was the vision again and they are amazed.

The news of the apparition traveled through the village and soon at least a good number of people joined. Among them, only two students from the convent can describe the vision. The priest urged others to pray and sing songs. With that, notable facts happened. Three hours passed before the vision disappeared completely. The message given on this occasion is as follows: "But pray, my children; God will answer you soon; my son is about to be moved."

Our Lady of Pellevoisin

Pellevoisin — France — 1876

A little about the psychic

Estela Faguette was born on September 12, 1839. Sweet and charming girl, she soon receives the religious and educational instructions needed in her childhood. At the age of eleven, something remarkable happened in her life: she was chosen by the community to carry the banner of Our Lady in the commemorative procession of the dogma of the Immaculate Conception. It was an exceptional moment that gave him joy and a closer relationship with the mother of God.

Three years later, she was forced to move to Paris searching for better living conditions for her family. At this time, he began to attend a convent which matures his devotion to Mary. He likes the environment so much that he ends up beginning the process of religious integration. For three consecutive years, he has done a fine job of preaching, also involving helping the neediest. At the end of this time, she is forced to leave her religious life and go to work with a family to help her parents.

In the hot season, their bosses move to the summer house located near Pellevoisin. Estela and her parents accompany them.

Estela's disease

Estela is seriously ill. Closer to the daughter, the maid's relatives provide the necessary emotional support for her at this time. His health is so delicate that his employers buy land in the city's cemetery. On the fourteenth of February, his personal doctor gives him the ultimatum: He has no more than a few hours to live. On this occasion, the girl has already resigned herself to her end. At least, she feels supported by her parents.

The cursed diseases that inflict suffering on him are: pulmonary tuberculosis, acute peritonitis and abdominal tumors. Months earlier, moved by her last hope of being cured, she had written a letter addressed to the Virgin Mary sent exactly to the cave dedicated to Our Lady of Lourdes. Here is the content of the letter:

"O my good Mother, here I am prostrate again at your feet. You cannot refuse to hear me. You have not forgotten that I am your daughter, that I love you. Grant me, therefore, through your divine Son, the health of the body, for your glory.

"Look at the pain of my parents, you know that they have nothing but me as a resource. Will I not be able to finish the work I started? If you cannot, because of my sins, get me a complete cure, you can at least get me a little strength to be able to earn my parents' life and that of me. You see, my good Mother, they are near having to beg for bread, I cannot think about it without being deeply distressed.

"Remember the sufferings you endured, on the night of the Savior's birth, when you were forced to go from door to door asking for asylum! Remember also what you suffered when Jesus was placed on the Cross! I have confidence in you, my good Mother, if you want, your Son can heal me. He knows that I very much wanted to be among the number of his wives and that it was to be pleasant that I sacrificed my existence for my family that needs me so much.

"Deign to listen to my pleas, my good Mother, and to pass them on to your divine Son. May He give me back my health if it pleases him, but let his will be done and not mine. May you at least grant me total resignation to your designs and may this serve my salvation and that of my parents. You have my heart, Holy Virgin, always keep it and let it be the pledge of my love and my recognition for your maternal goodness.

I promise you, my good Mother, if you grant me the graces that I ask of you, to achieve everything that depends on me for your glory and your divine Son.

"Take my dear niece under your protection and shelter her from bad examples. Do, O Holy Virgin, imitate you in your obedience and that one day I will be with you, Jesus, in eternity. "

Responding to this letter, the sequence of apparitions considered authentic by the Christian community began.

First apparition

February 14, 1876

It is the night of February 14, 1876. The servant of God is in a very fragile moment. Around midnight, a couple of figures appears at the edge of his bed. Follow the description of the seer herself: "Suddenly, the devil appeared beneath my bed. THE! How scared I was. It was horrible, I was making faces when the Virgin appeared on the other side of the bed ".

In this, the dialogue between them began:

"What are you doing here? Don't you see that Estela is dressed in my livery (scapular)? — Mary asked, referring to Satan.

"I came because I want to see you in your last moments." This gives me a lot of pleasure," Satan said sarcastically.

"Monster! Why do you act like that?" The maid asked.

"Because I am the devil, why balls," replied Satan.

"Calm down, my daughter." Do not be afraid of this monster," Mary asked.

"I am firmly convinced that I will be fine," said the patient.

"That's good! "Mary was glad."

The figures disappear into the darkness of the night without further explanation. This was the dying woman's first spiritual experience.

Second appearance

February 14, 1876

That same night, at dawn, The Virgin reappears showing herself with a worried and careful look towards her servant.

"I am here, my daughter." I want to hold you in my arms in the face of your fragility," announced the Immaculate.

"Thank you, my mother." However, I am still very disturbed by the sins that I committed in the past and that in my eyes were slight faults — commented the patient.

"The few good deeds and some fervent prayers that you addressed to me touched my mother's heart, I am full of mercy — Revealed our mother.

"These words reassure me," said the venerable Christian.

"Fortunately! I have three news to give you: For five consecutive days, I will see you; Saturday, you will die or be healed; if my son gives you his life, you will publish my glory," said Mary.

"I am touched." I beg you to tell me if I am going to be healed or not" Mary's devotee asked fervently.

"I agree." I received your letter and I say that it will be cured" said the Enlightened One.

"Glory to God and blessed are you among women." I don't know how to thank you for such grace.

"Do good always, and we are already rewarded." Take this difficult period as a test.

"I will take your advice," Estela promised.

"I am happy. Now go to sleep, my daughter.

That said, the mother of God disappeared in the middle of the dark night. Tired, the dying woman fell asleep feeling a little better. The next day would be another time of testing and purifying your soul.

Third apparition

February 15, 1876

Estela thought of all the events that had occurred in her brief life. Its existence had been a gathering of good and bad things with a pre-dominance of good facts. Then he thought: Why not die now in a state of grace?

As soon as the virgin appeared at the bedside, she set out to challenge that.

"Good night, my daughter." It's better? The virgin asked.

"A little better. My mother, with all due respect, if I had a choice, I would like to die while I am well-prepared — asked the dying woman.

"Ungrateful! If my Son gives you back your health, you need it. If my Son allowed himself to be touched, it was because of your great resignation and patience. Do not lose the fruit because of your choice — Sentenced the immaculate.

"Very sorry. I don't really know the father's designs. I accept with resignation to continue the mission." The servant demoted herself.

"I'm glad you thought about it." I leave my peace and happiness with you. Improvements!

That said, Mary rose to disappear completely. A wave of satisfaction and joy filled Estela's spirit. She had a lot to learn.

Fourth apparition

February 16, 1876

The devout Maryna has improved her health a little since her last appearances. Body and mind were reacting little by little even in the face of a highly dangerous disease. Who is like God? For him, nothing is impossible. Feeling satisfied, this venerable servant continued to receive visits from the Blessed Virgin Mary.

On the night of the respective day, she sat near the bed and got in touch again.

"My Blessed Virgin, why did you listen to me, a poor sinner?" Asked Estela.

"I'll explain." Those few good deeds and some fervent prayers that you dedicated to me touched my mother's heart; among others, that little letter that you wrote to me in September 1875. What touched me the most was this sentence: see my parents' pain if I missed them. They are near begging for bread. Remember that you also suffered when Jesus your Son was placed on the Cross. I showed this letter to my Son — revealed Mary.

"And what did he say? "Curiously Estela."

"That would heal you." In return, you should publish my glory," confirmed the mother of God.

"But how am I supposed to do it?" I'm not a big deal, I don't know how I could do that — Mary's servant was in doubt.

"I will enlighten you." Each thing at its time. Now rest, my daughter — Recommended the Enlightened One.

"Right. Thanks again — thanked the young woman.

Instantly, she was alone again with her ghosts. The future looked great and promising at this point.

Fifth appearance

February 17, 1876

It was an ordinary night like any other. Suddenly, the figure of Mary appeared, approaching with her usual smile.

"I am here to remind you of your obligations since you are a little better," Mary said.

"As soon as I am completely improved, I promise to fulfill them all," the servant assured her.

"I am happy. Do you want to be my faithful devotee?" Mary asked.

"What should I do? Asked Estela.

"If you want to serve me, be simple and let your actions prove your words," the saint said.

"What if I move somewhere else?" "The devotee questioned."

"Wherever you are, whatever you do, you can earn blessings and proclaim my glory," Mary said.

Pausing, the mother of God was saddened a little and then continued:

"What saddens me most is seeing that people have no respect for my son in the Eucharist and the way people pray while their minds are on other things. I say this to those who pretend to be godly.

"Can I immediately proclaim your glory?" — Estela asked.

"Yea! Yes, but first ask your confessor what he thinks. You will encounter obstacles; you will be provoked and people will say that you are crazy. However, do not pay attention to them. Be true to me and I will help you — Said the Virgin.

The Immaculate has disappeared like smoke. There followed a period of excitement, suffering, and pain for the patient. At exactly 12:30 he felt better. In the evening, his confessor revealed the apparitions. Following her advice, she attended the later mass where she was completely healed. Blessed be our holy Mother!

Sixth apparition

July 1, 1876

Estela resumed her normal activities. In particular, I was engaged in promoting our lady's devotion as a form of gratitude for her healing. In this activity, he felt happy, fulfilled and with an indescribable peace.

After the normal day's work, this servant was gathered in her room in prayer. Around ten o'clock at night, the virgin appeared surrounded by light.

"Be calm, my daughter, patience, it will be difficult for you, but I am with you," the Enlightened One assured.

The devoted servant was in such a state of ecstasy that she was unable to respond. The mother of God remained there for a few moments and when saying goodbye said:

"Courage, I must return.

Rising to the heavens, Mary blessed him. The maid kept thinking about all the events. Later, he surrendered to tiredness by going to sleep.

Seventh appearance

July 2, 1876

The days were very busy for this sweet young man. Although she was always busy with her duties, she kept thinking about the apparitions and what they represented in her life. So, he did not wait for the night to come and find his beloved mother again.

At 10:30 am, went to bed hoping to see another paranormal vision. Although, she was so tired that she fell asleep. An hour later he woke up and said his usual prayers. That was when he was visited again by the blessed mother of God.

"I am satisfied with your work." Through you, many sinners will be converted to a new life. Go on, my son won more souls who devoted themselves to him more deeply. His heart is so full of love for my heart, that he can never refuse me anything. For me, it will touch and soften the hardest hearts," confided the Virgin Mary.

"I ask you for a sign." My good mother, please, for your glory," requested the servant.

"And isn't your healing a great proof of my power?" I came specially to save sinners," said Mary.

"Yes, it is true, my mother," agreed the devotee.

"About miracles, let the people see this," concluded Mary.

That said, the enlightened one disappeared without further explanation. Today's job was done. Exhausted, the servant of God fell asleep again.

Eighth apparition

July 3, 1876

Mary's maid was in reflection in her room when she again received a visit from the queen of heaven. This time, she was as beautiful as the other times.

"I want you to be calmer, more peaceful, I didn't say what day or time I will return, but you need to rest," the Virgin scolded him.

Before Mary's servant could answer and show how she really felt before the great mission presented, the virgin smiled at her and concluded:

"I came to end the party."

The vision then evaporated. Each of these visions was creating a kind of interesting film for the entire Catholic community. It was an honor for that young girl to be the protagonist of all these revelations. He would therefore continue his work.

Ninth apparition

September 9, 1876

Our beloved friend, servant, was praying the rosary in her room when she saw the vision again. Our lady appeared in the figure of a beautiful woman. Looking around, the apparition found:

"You deprived me of my visit on the fifteenth of August because you were not calm enough." You have a true French character: They want to know everything before they learn and understand everything before they know it. I could have gone back, you deprived me of my visit because I was waiting for an act of submission and obedience from you.

"I wasn't feeling ready." Better late than never, right? The servant asked.

"Yes, you're right. Keep looking after my sheep," recommended the Virgin.

That said, he looked up at the skies and disappeared instantly. Her venerable devotee was happy for this meeting after so long.

Tenth apparition

September 10, 1876

On this day, the mother of God appeared to Saint Estela at about the same time the other day. There were only a few moments when she stayed in the room to say:

"They must pray. I will give you an example.

In the next instant, she put her hands together and waved goodbye. Then the maid went to rest from her long jobs throughout the day. However, she was satisfied with the results of her efforts.

Eleventh appearance

September 15, 1876

It was five long days when the seer was at an internal spiritual retreat. Reconciling work and religious life, the young woman felt completely fulfilled in her purposes. But it seemed that there was a block in his life. It was because of this that the Virgin appeared to him again.

As always, he had the vision in a moment of reflection and prayer in his room. Fully enlightened, Mary showed a sad and worried countenance to the servant.

"Good night, my lady, how nice of you to come." I was thinking about all the facts in my life. I concluded that I lived a perverse dark night that persecutes me until today — Estela verified.

"You need to get over it." It is true that he made many mistakes. But his letter and his regrets made a miracle possible. It is now up to you to continue your life with more optimism — Mary said.

"I hope to do it." What about the faithful in the country? The servant asked.

"I can't stop my son anymore." I have already made all my efforts at my fingertips," stressed the Immaculate.

"What is going to happen then?" "Interestingly, the maid."

"France is going to suffer," the beautiful woman announced.

"That sad!" She observed the young woman.

"Have courage and confidence." He supported the apparition.

"If I said that, maybe no one will believe me," thought the psychic.

"I say in advance, all the worse for those who do not believe, they will recognize the truth of my words later," announced Mary.

That said, the mother of God disappeared leaving her confidant even more amazed by those facts. It was truly an honor to participate in these important moments. I would therefore continue on the mission.

Twelfth apparition

November 1, 1876

It was the day of all the saints. It had been a long time since the last appearance, which made our dear friend a little sad and bored. The experience of the visions was so intense and good that she always wanted to repeat it and that is what happened on this day.

Appearing in an ordinary way, with her arms outstretched and wearing the scapular, the mother of God looked around and looked toward the horizon with a sigh. Then he smiled broadly, giving the servant a look of kindness. Then he disappeared without explanation. It was enough to fill that sweet young woman's day of happiness.

Thirteenth appearance

November 5, 1876

Estela was just finishing praying the rosary when she saw the Blessed Virgin.

"Oh, ma'am." I feel unworthy of the mission you proposed to me because there are so many people more qualified than I am to proclaim your glory — thought the servant.

"I choose you. I chose the gentle and gentle for my glory. Be brave, your task is about to begin — said the beautiful lady, smiling.

Afterwards, the Blessed Virgin crossed her hands and disappeared into the immensity of the night.

Fourteenth apparition

November 11, 1876

For a few days, this special servant of Our Lady repeatedly engaged in prayers seeking inspiration and help from heaven in resolving her most critical doubts. At one point, she cried out the following sentence:

"Remember me, Most Holy Virgin Mary.

Immediately, the beautiful lady appeared with a beautiful smile.

"You didn't waste your time today, you worked for me," he said.

"Do you mean the Scapular I made?" The girl asked.

"Yea. My wish is for you to do many," confirmed Mary.

An unsettling silence hung between the two. The virgin's expression suddenly changed from joy to sadness. He concluded by recommending:

"Courage!

Handling the scapular and folding his hands, his spirit disappeared. Now, her devoted beloved would be left alone with her duties.

Last appearance

December 8, 1876

It had been almost a month since the beloved virgin had appeared to his devoted servant. This fact made her distressed and thoughtful. She kept thinking about it at the Mass she attended. Upon returning home and staying in the privacy of her room, she appeared gloriously for what would be the last time.

"My daughter, do you remember my words?" The virgin asked.

Suddenly, the most important words of the virgin came to the fore especially about the devotion of the Scapular and other secrets.

"Yes, I remember it perfectly, my mother," confirmed the servant.

"Repeat those words many times. They will help you during your trials and tribulations. You won't see me anymore," said Mary.

"What must become of me, most holy mother?" "The devotee was desperate.

"I will be with you, but invisible," he comforted her.

"I saw lines of people pushing against me and threatening me, it made me petrified," Estela said.

"You need not be afraid of them, I chose you to announce my glory and to spread this devotion," Our Lady said.

Mary held the scapular in her hands. The image was so encouraging that the servant had an idea.

"My beloved mother, could you please give me this scapular?"

"Come and kiss him," Mary consented.

Approaching, the maid had the pleasure of touching and kissing the sacred relic which became the most important moment of her life. The conversation continued.

"You yourself, go to Prelaat and present him with the model you made and tell him that if he helps you, it pleases me more than watching my children use it while they walk away from everything that insults my people, while my son receives the sacrament of his love and does everything possible to repair the damage that is already done. See the graces that I must bestow on everyone who uses to have confidence in me and at the same time spread this devotion — Mary spoke.

Extending her hands, the saint caused an abundant rain to fall. She continued:

"The graces that my son grants you are: Health, trust, respect, love, holiness and all the other graces that exist. He refuses me anything.

"Mom, what should I put on the other side of the scapular?"

"I have that side reserved for me," replied Jesus' mother.

The tone was goodbye. A sadness flooded the environment knowing that this was the last contact on earth between the two.

"Courage, if he doesn't do what he wants, go higher." Do not be afraid. I'll help you," Mary recommended.

As he strolled around the room, his spirit flew and disappeared through the cracks in the room. This sequence of apparitions was ended. Blessed be our mother!

Our Lady of Knock

Ireland

August 21, 1879

Knock was a small village with about ten houses. The apparition took place on a stormy and cold night: Exactly on the back wall of the chapel appeared three gorgeous people and an altar. Two hundred people were at the scene now and could testify that Mary, Joseph, and St. John the Evangelist were there. The visions were repeated on other occasions and due to the occurrence of miracles related to the fact, they were taken for granted by the Catholic Church.

Appearances in China

Our Lady of Dong-Lu

1900

China has always been a stage of resistance to the expansion of Christianity. However, Our Lady always seeks the conversion of her children. A miraculous event took place in June 1900. At the time, Christian persecutors surrounded Dong Lu's hometown on the verge of exterminating the resisters. That was when the Immaculate appeared surrounded by angels. This was enough to terrify opponents and make them run stampede.

Saved from danger, the residents built a temple in honor of Mary as a way of thanking them. Then, the sanctuary was recognized as an official pilgrimage center, a feast day was given in honor of Our Lady and finally, the country's consecration to the bosom of the Virgin Mother.

China's communist regime was the main antagonist for the growth of Christianity in the region. Feeling threatened, the said government gathered a troop of five thousand soldiers in addition to dozens of armored cars and helicopters attacking the Marian sanctuary. The action resulted in the confiscation of the statue of the Virgin Mary and the arrest of many priests.

Taken as an illegal religion, Christianity is continuously persecuted in China. Christians in the region tend to exercise religiosity in a secret way to avoid retaliation. Still, many of them have disappeared or been arrested. It is the real battle of good against evil.

One thing that saddened the Catholic people of the world was when the Communists destroyed the Dong-Lu Church during the Beijing Olympics. However, the Image of Our Lady of China was left intact as it was not found by the anti-Christians.

Our Lady is also queen of China. Even if Satan continues his persecution, there will be no shortage of Catholics in what is the most populous country in the world. Proof of this are the countless apparitions reported in Dong-Lu. Let us pray for all our Chinese brothers and sisters of faith.

Our Lady of Qing Yang

1900

There was a peasant woman from this region who was very sick. She went to all the doctors she knew. However, no recommended treatment had any effect.

Once, he was walking in the countryside when a beautiful lady wearing a long white dress and a blue sash appeared on the way.

"Collect grass from this area. Make tea and drink. I promise your cure soon.

"Okay, madam." I will do as you ask.

The peasant woman obeyed the order given by gathering herbs from there. Upon returning home, he drank tea. As promised, it improved in a short time. She only discovered who the beautiful apparition was about when she saw the same image portrayed in the home of a

Catholic. In this, the news spread throughout the region and throughout the country.

Due to the circumstances, the diocese took over the purchase of the land on which the saint had appeared, in sequence building a chapel and later a church. Over time, the pilgrimage to the place only increased and consolidated itself as one of the most important Marian temples in the world.

Our Lady of Sheshan

Shanghai-china-1900

Shanghai is located on the east coast of China. Due to its strategic position, next to the Yangzi River valley, it became the gateway for Catholic missionaries with the aim of evangelizing China. As soon as they settled in the country, they built a shrine dedicated to Our Lady of Sheshan in the west of the city. Next to it, a retreat house was also built to house the retired Jesuits.

Our Lady's great achievement in the region was that she saved the diocese from the attack promoted by the Taiping rebellion. As a thank you, the local Christians erected a basilica in honor of the mother of God, making her the special protector of the Shanghai diocese.

With the holding of the first bishops' conference, the image of Shanghai was adopted as Our Lady Queen of China. Due to the Cultural Revolution, the original image of Our Lady was destroyed and another image was replaced in April 2000. A copy of this statue was given to Pope Benedict XVI and named "Our Lady of Sheshan". This is one of the most important Marian centers in the country where the saint truly crushes the serpent's head, representing the victory of good over evil.

END

Lightning Source UK Ltd.
Milton Keynes UK
UKHW051804210922
409198UK00012B/793